For Emma D. Dryden,
visionary friend, extraordinaire…
Thank you.
—C.L.

Great Polar Bear

Written and Illustrated by Carolyn Lesser

Great polar bear…

how do you survive

on the thick ice covering the deep Arctic Sea?

As you pad through storms,
veils of snow
race past your fringy paws.

Time to scoop
a drift hollow…

huddle in,

back to the icy blast, nose pushed under the snow, paws snuggling your body.

Winds howl…snow swirls,
covering you like dust
until you vanish.

Sleep warm, polar bear.

The earth leans far from the sun
as you rouse from your drift-bed
this winter solstice morning.

How lucky that every other day of the year
each hollow hair of your fur
gathers sunlight
to heat your black skin and thick layer of fat.

Your blubbery blanket keeps you warm
for long, dog-paddling swims
and months of day-and-night
winter wandering.

As you wander, great bear,
your keen nose smells
bear friends and relatives nearby.
some nap behind hills of ice.

Others travel, like you, comforted
by the scent of companions
all on singular journeys…
alone, but not lonely.

Climbing a mountain of wind-piled pack ice,
your hind feet step neatly into footprints
made by your front paws.
You stand on top, stretching twelve feet tall,
sniffing the air and the Arctic Sea.
Seals are near.

You clamber down, rush toward the scent,
pacing over smooth ice
on gritty paws that never slip.
As you near the snow-covered mound,
your footfalls slow, silenced
by fur between your paw pads.

Flopping on your belly,
you glide downwind of the dome
over the seal's breathing hole.
Pushing with hind legs,
pulling with front claws,
you inch closer...closer...stop.

Silent as light,
still as fallen snow,
you wait all day

for a seal to breathe.

Great polar bear,
you have fooled the seal
swimming under you.
He surfaces and gulps for air.
Your paws, heavy as sledgehammers,
smash the ice dome.

Your mouth grabs the seal, jerks it up, out.
You feast for hours on skin and blubber,
stopping often for a snow bath.
Finished, you nap. The carcass waits
for those who follow in twilight or darkness.

Mothers with cubs,
young bears, and foxes
need the meat you leave.

They depend
on your planning,
your power.

Great polar bear, what calls you
to journey far across boundless ice?

Mighty northwest winds
cause ice to drift east,
pile high, collapse.
Landmarks are ever changing.
What tells you to wander west?
How do you know your boundaries?

And when you find a female's scent,
nothing will stop your race to her.

Crossing ice and open ocean
in a straight line,
you travel as far as you must,
battle if you must, to mate with her.

Then you go on,
never knowing the cubs
she will bring from her den
into spring sunshine.
Perhaps one will grow strong
like you, polar bear.

Strong polar bear, in a golden sunrise
the snow goose and gander huddle on their nest,
spring gale snow piling to their heads.
Fat from winter kills, you waddle past
their peering eyes, leaving wide tracks.

You follow retreating sea ice into deep bays,
stride over softening ice like a skater,
sprawl as it bends under your weight.

Each day the sun rises higher,
carving solid ice into islands.
You leap from one floe to another,
swim farther, longer.

When you are overheated and tired,
you haul out, shake dry,
and nap on an ice pillow, drifting for miles.

Suddenly you wake, sniff, stand, look.
A seal sleeps on the edge of the ice,
looks up, and sleeps again.
You slip into the water, head first,
as if poured into the sea.

Stalking, you hang motionless as an ice floe,
only eyes, nose, and ears above water,
front paws paddling, back paws steering.

Without sound or splash,
you slink under water, under ice.
Webbed paws big as plates
pull strong, glide you
into forests of kelp hiding starfish,
shrimp, worms, and anemones.

Whoosh! You rocket from the sea,
strike the seal dead in one blow, one bite.

You hunt every spring day to store fat.
Seals are scarce. Winds are warming.
One day ice islands soften...sag...
surrender to seawater.

Great polar bear,
summer light casts long shadows.
Ice and seals are gone.

You come ashore, wander the capes
and headlands in cool offshore breezes,
follow tracks to meet other bears.

All nod friendliness,
circle, nuzzle muzzles.

A young male challenges you,
then another and another.
You play-fight one at a time,
never growling or biting hard.

They learn to fight for a mate,
fight only when necessary,
for in the harsh Arctic,
severe injury means certain death.

After the lesson, hot and exhausted,
you flop on the cool gravel beach
with the young bears and nap.

Brave polar bear, the summer sun
is your most powerful enemy,
more dangerous than the icy winter wind.
Melting ice holds no seals.
Your stored fat must keep you alive.

You slow to walking
hibernation,
amble to munch berries,
nibble sparse beach grass and kelp,
struggle to catch an elusive squirrel
or lemming...an eider duck
swimming in the bay.

To cool off you swim and pant and sprawl
or roll over, waving your legs in the breeze
so heat can escape from your foot pads
and belly.

You excavate a bed in the permafrost.
Hidden in a thicket of willows,
protected from the sun, you sleep.
Life happens in slow motion.

It is time to wait...
to watch.

Restless polar bear,
as days pass,
you shuffle along the beach
sniffing, watching, listening.
The sea and air tell you fall is coming.

Your tracks are narrow,
hungry, thin bear.

Each morning you pace faster,
taste cold sea air,
watch an oily crust of ice
form on the still water
of tidal ponds.

Daylight hours are shorter.
Swans take flight.

Snow falls.

Every day is colder, the wind bolder.
Fierce winds crush ice crystals,
whip them into a thick soup.
Snow and slush freeze together.
Chunks and clumps collide.

Listen.
The ice is alive.
What does it tell you, polar bear?

Bays fill with sheets of ice.
Rocked by tides and currents,
Ice sheets crash, break…
into gigantic floating ice lily pads.

Eager to hunt, you step on them, crash through.
Perhaps tomorrow, great bear.

Hungry polar bear,
as you awaken this day,
mist clouds the air.
Seal smells call you back
to your native ice.

Tides and currents and winds lift, push, pull.
Ice grinds, bends, booms, snap-cracks.
Fierce snow squalls blur land and sky.
Arctic gale winds tousle your fur.

Gingerly you test the ice again,
each step sounding like one long beat
of a high-pitched kettle drum.
The sea ice holds.

On a head swinging dead run,
you race to meet your kingdom
of endless ice.

Freeze-up has come at last.

Polar bear, alone
in the vast Arctic night,
are you ready for your journey?

Clouds sail clear of the moon
and swirls of snow glow on the ice
as you pace through pools of moonlight.

The waving curtains of light are beckoning,
weaving ribbons of color through stars.
The aurora borealis is your companion this night.

Some say the lights are the spirits of the old ones,
the ones who have gone before.

Their spirit-light will watch over you,
the great Nanuq, the one who is without shadow,
the mightiest of all.

Within you are the secrets of cold and alone.
Bon voyage, great polar bear.

Explorer's Notes

When scientists, field zoologists, and local people observe polar bears, they record their findings in journals or on film, or they tell others what they have seen. Some write detailed reports to share their discoveries with other scientists. Here are recent observations and findings.

Kids and adults must live as brave environmental conservationists, standing out and speaking up on behalf of the health of our planet, to stop global warming.

Ice + seals = polar bears

Seals are the major food source of polar bears. Neither seals nor polar bears can survive without a healthy arctic ecosystem and perfect weather for creating ideal ice. Ideal ice is a solid cover of ice that forms early in autumn and remains solid until late spring.

Ideal ice gives seals enough time to have their young and for the young to grow strong enough to feed themselves. Ideal ice gives bears a long time to hunt seals through autumn, winter, and spring, storing enough fat to live through the dangerous hot summer, when seals are hard to find, hunt, catch, and eat.

Imperfect ice forms in late autumn, covers less area, and thaws in the early spring. Seals do not have enough time to raise their pups, and polar bears do not have enough time to fatten up. Both populations suffer when ice conditions are imperfect.

The environment is changing

In the 1980s, the Western Hudson Bay polar bear population was 1,200 to 1,500 bears. The weather and habitat were perfect. On ideal ice, female bears had two or three cubs. The cubs grew fast, many independent before two years of age. Free of their cubs, females could breed again and produce more healthy bears.

In the 1990s, the polar bear population dropped to 600 to 800. The warming weather made imperfect ice, and bears and seals did not have enough time on ice. In the early 2000s, the continual warming weather caused late freeze-up and early thawing. Fewer cubs were born, and bears were smaller and thinner.

Now, there are years of ideal ice and years of imperfect ice, and although stable, polar bear populations have not returned to their highest numbers. Bears are still smaller, and fewer cubs are born every three years—not two.

Global warming

Today, polar bears are not on the endangered list but are considered threatened and vulnerable due to the loss of sea ice wordwide. From long-range scientific studies, it is clear that global warming and its effect on the formation of ice is the most serious threat to the lives of polar bears and seals. In 2017, the worldwide population of bears is closer to 23,000, rather than 25,000 in the 1990s.

Scientists and people who live and work around polar bears have noticed changes in summer patterns of bears. Polar bears do not sleep as much in the summer. They hunt different prey, such as beluga whales and geese, and they eat more berries. These food sources are not enough to sustain a polar bear through the summer.

Polar bears can adapt to a changing habitat, but they cannot adapt quickly. It may take generations for bears to adapt to a warming world.

Sources
Ian Thorleifson, field zoologist in Churchill, MT
Alysa McCall, Director of Conservation Outreach, Staff Scientist, Polar Bears International

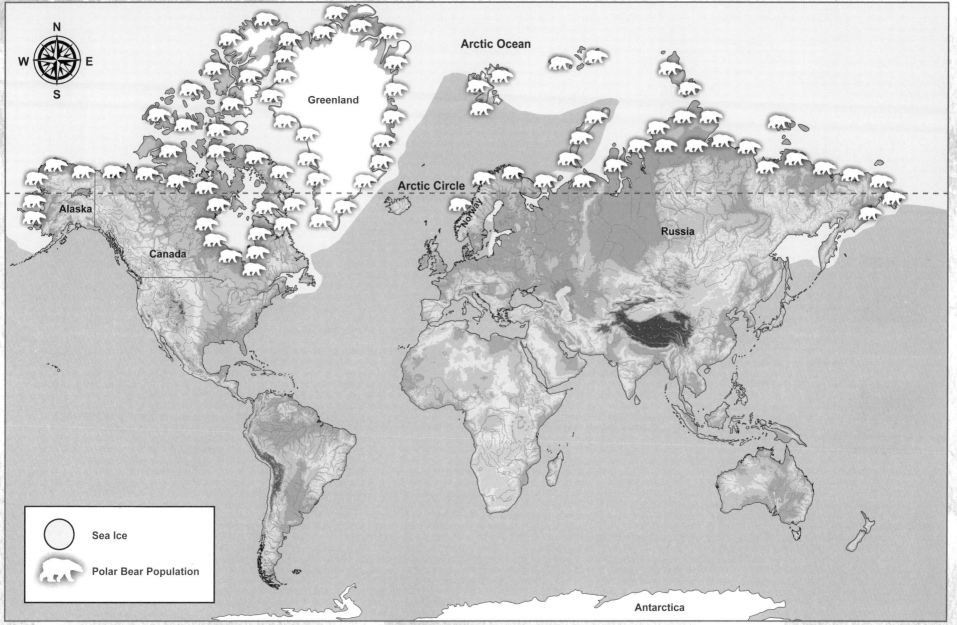

Polar bear populations are found only in the far North, following the edges of continents where sea ice supports seal populations.

The bears in this book live in Canada in the Southwest Hudson Bay colony, the southernmost population of polar bears.

There are no polar bears in Antarctica.

Author's Journal

Early afternoon. Arctic twilight. Our tundra buggy caravan arrives at Cape Churchill, a stationary train-hotel, for tomorrow's explorations. I stand at a buggy window, binoculars searching.

"Across the pond— a sleeping bear," I gasp.

Ian, our field zoologist and driver, says, "Big male."

I pull down the top window with a laser focus on the bear. "Come to us," I murmur.

The bear lifts his head, looks, stands, shakes, slides onto the pond, shuffles across. Close...closer...below my window. He stands, his huge paws rocking the buggy. I lean into the chill and whisper, "Hello, bear. You are magnificent." His black mouth opens wide and..."Haaaaaaaaaaaa." His hot, fishy bear breath clouds my grin. We gaze into each other's eyes. Time stops.

The magnificence, power, and grace of wildness in that polar bear is in every remembrance of my five Arctic winters and one Arctic Circle summer. These remembrances informed every word and shred of hand-painted, cut paper in this book.

I fell in love with planet Earth as a very curious small child and now write and illustrate as an adventurous exploring author-illustrator living in St. Louis, MO.

—Carolyn Lesser

Brimming with creative inspiration, how-to projects, and useful information to enrich your everyday life, Quarto Knows is a favorite destination for those pursuing their interests and passions. Visit our site and dig deeper with our books into your area of interest: Quarto Creates, Quarto Cooks, Quarto Homes, Quarto Lives, Quarto Drives, Quarto Explores, Quarto Gifts, or Quarto Kids.

© 2018 Quarto Publishing Group USA Inc.
Text © 1996, 2018 Carolyn Lesser
Illustrations © 2018 Carolyn Lesser
Originally published in 1996 as *Great Crystal Bear* (978-0-15200-667-9)

Published in 2018 by Seagrass Publishing, an imprint of The Quarto Group.
6 Orchard Road, Suite 100, Lake Forest, CA 92630, USA.
T (949) 380-7510 **F** (949) 380-7575 **www.QuartoKnows.com**

Seagrass Press titles are also available at discount for retail, wholesale, promotional, and bulk purchase. For details, contact the Special Sales Manager by email at specialsales@quarto.com or by mail at The Quarto Group, Attn: Special Sales Manager, 401 Second Avenue North, Suite 310, Minneapolis, MN 55401 USA.

ISBN: 978-1-63322-502-2

Digital edition published in 2018
eISBN: 978-1-63322-503-9

Printed in China
10 9 8 7 6 5 4 3 2 1

Acknowledgments
With a grateful heart for Josalyn Moran and Patricia Brigandi, championing editors and friends, and the Quarto talents: April Balotro-Carothers and Shelley Baugh.

For the Arctic guys: Dan, Ian, Bill, and Nikita—great friends of bears and me.

And for my always cheering cheerleaders: my children and their children, and Carol Kujawa, Larry Shles, Daryl Shankland, Diane Scolley, Fred Lewis, Joann Radil, Katherine Ziegler, Martha La Fata, Beth Tabbert, Jennifer Gille, Judy Hergert, Shirley Aschinger, Judith Heil, Mary Jordan, and Goranna and Sasha Maybury.

And remembered empowering encouragement from my teachers Min Wegener, Mildred Leyda, Wes McNair, and Dr. Norman Frenzel.
Thank you.
—C.L.